John R. Robinson

In the District Court of the Fourth Judicial District of the

State of California

John R. Robinson

In the District Court of the Fourth Judicial District of the State of California

ISBN/EAN: 9783337414740

Printed in Europe, USA, Canada, Australia, Japan

Cover: Foto ©Suzi / pixelio.de

More available books at **www.hansebooks.com**

IN THE

District Court of the Fourth Judicial District,

OF THE STATE OF CALIFORNIA,

IN AND FOR THE CITY AND COUNTY OF SAN FRANCISCO.

———————•———————

JOHN R. ROBINSON,

Plaintiff,

vs.

THE CENTRAL PACIFIC RAILROAD COMPANY OF CALIFORNIA ET ALS.

Defendants.

COMPLAINT.

ALFRED A. COHEN,
DELOS LAKE,

Attorneys for Plaintiff

In the District Court

OF THE

FOURTH JUDICIAL DISTRICT

OF THE STATE OF CALIFORNIA,

In and for the City and County of San Francisco.

John R. Robinson, Plaintiff,

vs.

The Central Pacific Railroad Company of California, Leland Stanford, Collis P. Huntington, Mark Hopkins, Charles Crocker, Charles Crocker, Executor of the estate of Edwin B. Crocker deceased ; Charles Marsh, Edward H. Miller Jr., B. B. Redding, Wells, Fargo & Co., James B. Haggin, David D. Colton, The Contract and Finance Company, The Southern Pacific Railroad Company, The Market Street Railway Company, The Potrero and Bay View Railroad Company, The California Pacific Railroad Company, The Los Angeles and San Pedro Railroad Company, The Rocky Mountain Coal and Iron Company, of Wyoming ; C. H. Cummings, Robert Robinson, Silas W. Sanderson, Atlantic and Pacific Telegraph Company, The Western Development Company, The San Francisco and San Jose Railroad Company, The San Joaquin Valley Railroad Company, The California and Oregon Railroad Company, The Sacramento Publishing Company, William H. Mills, The Central Pacific Railroad Company, John Doe, Richard Roe, Alexander Foe, and Richard Joe, the names of four last named defendants being unknown to plaintiff, Defendants.

1.

Plaintiff above named complaining against the above named defendants, avers, that this action is brought against said defendants on behalf of this plaintiff and all other stockholders of the Central Pacific Railroad Company, of California, who may choose to come in and contribute to the cost and expense of this action.

2.

That the defendant, the Central Pacific Railroad Company of California, was duly organized and incorporated under the laws of the State of California, on or about the 27th day of June, 1861, and since that day has continued to be and is a corporation for the purposes mentioned and enumerated in Articles of Association, a copy whereof is hereto annexed, marked A, and made a part of this complaint, and is the same corporation mentioned and referred to as the Central Pacific Railroad Company of California, in a law of the Congress of the United States, entitled, "An Act to aid in the construction of a Railroad and Telegraph line from the Missouri River to the Pacific Ocean, and to secure to the Government the use of the same for postal, military, and other purposes," passed July 1st, 1862, and another act, passed July 2d, 1864, to amend said last mentioned act, and subsequent acts and resolutions supplemental to, and amendatory of, said first mentioned act, and to which said acts, laws and resolutions, and every part thereof, the plaintiffs refer as a part of this complaint.

That said Central Pacific Railroad Company of California heretofore duly accepted, acted upon, complied with, and is now acting upon and under the said laws, acts, and resolutions hereinbefore mentioned and referred to.

3.

That whenever hereafter, in this complaint, the Central Pacific Railroad Company of California is mentioned, and intended to be mentioned, it is designated by the letters C. P.

4.

That one of the principal places of business of said C. P. is, and has been for over one year last past, in said city and county of San Francisco, and during said last mentioned period frequent business meetings of its directors have been held in said city and county.

5.

That the capital stock of said C. P. is, and has been, since the organization and incorporation thereof, the sum of eight million five hundred thousand dollars, divided into eighty-five thousand (85,000) shares, of one hundred dollars each.

6.

That on the 15th day of April, 1862, the plaintiff duly subscribed for, and has heretofore, in good faith, paid for to said C. P., at the nominal par value thereof, ten shares of the capital stock of said C. P., and has, ever since said 15th day of April, held and owned, and now holds and owns said ten shares.

7.

That the defendants, Leland Stanford, C. P. Huntington, Mark Hopkins, Charles Crocker, and Charles Marsh originally sub-

scribed to said capital stock, and agreed to take and pay for the
shares thereof so subscribed by them respectively, at their par value as follows, to wit:

Said Leland Stanford, 150 shares.

Said C. P. Huntington, 150 shares.

Said Mark Hopkins, 150 shares.

Said Charles Crocker, 150 shares.

And said Charles Marsh, 50 shares.

That afterward, but at what particular date or dates plaintiff
is ignorant, all the shares of the capital stock, so as aforesaid
subscribed for by said last named defendants, purport to have been
issued by said last mentioned corporation to said last mentioned
defendants respectively.

The plaintiff is informed and believes, and therefore avers, upon
and according to his information and belief, that said last named
defendants did not, nor did either of them, ever pay to said corporation, or deliver to it, any money or other valuable thing for the
shares of capital stock so purporting to have been issued to said last
named defendants, respectively; but in truth and in fact the whole
of such stock was so issued without any consideration ever having
been paid or delivered therefor, illegally, in fraud and violation of
the statute in such case made and provided, and in fraud of the
rights of the plaintiff and the other stockholders of the C. P.

That the only stock of said last mentioned corporation ever paid
for in good faith, according to law, and lawfully issued by it, is and
has been such shares as are now held by the plaintiff, and such
shares as were heretofore issued to the county of Placer, State
of California, to wit, twenty-five hundred shares; to the county of
Sacramento, State aforesaid, three thousand shares; to Samuel
Hooper, fifty shares; to Benj. T. Reid, fifty shares; to Glidden &
Williams, composed of Wm. J. Glidden, Jno. A. Glidden, John M.
Glidden, and John M. S. Williams, one hundred and twenty-five
shares; Orville D. Lambard, one hundred and twenty shares;
Charles A. Lambard, two hundred shares; Mrs. Anne F. Judah,
twenty-five shares; Samuel P. Shaw, fifty shares; R. O. Ives,
twenty-five shares; Samuel Brannan, two hundred shares; and about
nine hundred shares issued to divers individuals whose names and
residences are unknown to plaintiff.

That the said last mentioned defendants and their confederates, to the plaintiff unknown, assuming to act and in fact but illegally acting as directors of said C. P., and composing a majority thereof, have caused to be issued to themselves and divers their confederates, to plaintiff unknown, large amounts of the capital stock of said corporation; but that all of said stock so issued to them and their said confederates has been issued without consideration illegally and fraudulently, and the issuance thereof was and is wholly illegal and void.

8.

That nearly all of the aforesaid stock so as aforesaid issued to the County of Placer—to wit, 2,500 shares; to the County of Sacramento, 3,000 shares; to Samuel Hooper, fifty shares; to Benjamin T. Reid, fifty shares; to Glidden & Williams, 125 shares; to Orville D. Lambard, 120 shares; to Charles A. Lambard, 200 shares; to Mrs. Anne F. Judah, twenty-five shares; to Samuel P. Shaw, fifty shares; to R. O. Ives, twenty-five shares; to Samuel Brannan, 200 shares; and a portion of the other 900 shares or thereabouts as above mentioned—has been purchased by the defendants, Leland Stanford, C. P. Huntington, Mark Hopkins, Charles and E. B. Crocker, and who now claim to own the same; and plaintiff is informed and believes, and so avers, upon and according to his information and belief, that said purchase was made and paid for by said Stanford, Huntington, Hopkins, Charles and E. B. Crocker, with moneys derived by them from the earnings of the said C. P. under the name of a certain firm known as Charles Crocker & Company and a certain corporation known as the Contract and Finance Company, as will be hereafter shown, and not otherwise.

9.

That the defendants Leland Stanford, Charles Crocker, Charles Marsh, C. P. Huntington, Mark Hopkins, and others their confcderates, to plaintiff unknown, were the directors of said C. P. to manage the concerns thereof, for the first three months after the organization thereof. That at the expiration of said three months, the defendants Leland Stanford, Charles Crocker, E. B. Crocker, C. P. Huntington, Mark Hopkins, and Charles Marsh, and their confederates, to plaintiff unknown, pretending, appearing, and falsely claiming to be the nominal owners of a majority of the capital stock of said C. P., purporting to have been issued by it, and by other secret devices and contrivances unknown to plaintiff, combining and confederating together, elected themselves a majority of the directors of said last mentioned corporation, and have from thence hitherto, as nominal directors thereof, exercised the entire control and management of all its affairs, business, subsidies, and assets, to their joint and individual benefit, advantage, profit, and gain, and to the loss, detriment, and disadvantage of said last mentioned corporation, of plaintiff and the other stockholders thereof, as hereinafter more particularly averred and charged.

10.

Plaintiff avers that he is advised, informed, and believes, and therefore, upon and according to his information and belief, avers, that neither of the said defendants Leland Stanford, Hopkins, Huntington, Charles and E. B. Crocker, or their confederates, although they claim to be respectively, and assert they are respectively, and nominally appear to be respectively, owners of a large number of shares of the capital stock of said C. P., over and above what they respectively purport to have subscribed for, at the time of the organization of said C. P., yet, in truth and in fact, as plaintiff is informed and believes, and therefore avers upon and according to his nformation and belief, all such shares not so as aforesaid subscribed for, have in part been purchased and acquired by said last mentioned defendants and their confederates, with the assets, moneys, and property of said last mentioned corporation, and in part issued to said defendants and their confederates without any compensation moving to said last mentioned corporation; in violation of the statute under which said corporation was organized and is acting; and all such shares are held in trust by said last named defendants for said corporation.

11.

That in and by the Act of Congress first aforesaid, and the acts and resolutions supplemental to and amendatory thereof, the said defendant C. P. was and is authorized and empowered to construct, and maintain a railroad and telegraph line from the Pacific Coast, at or near San Francisco, California, to Echo City, in the Territory of Utah, in and through all the intervening States and Territories, a distance of seven hundred and eighty-four and one-half miles, or thereabouts.

That in and by said acts and resolutions last above mentioned, there was granted to said C. P. by the United States of America, the right of way for the railroad and telegraph line of said last named corporation, for the distance aforesaid, over and through the public lands of the United States, situate between San Francisco aforesaid and Echo City aforesaid, including all necessary grounds for stations, buildings, workshops, depots, machine-shops, switches, side tracks, turn-tables, and water stations, and the right to take from the public lands adjacent to the line of its said road for the construction thereof such earth, stone, timber, and other material as might be necessary therefor; and also twenty alternate sections of public land, (not including mineral lands containing the precious metals) for each and every mile of its said road on the line thereof, and within the limits of twenty miles on each side of said road, equal to twelve thousand eight hundred acres of public land per mile of said railroad; and also the timber on all mineral lands within said limits.

And there was further granted to it, the said corporation, the C. P., and the Secretary of the Treasury of the United States was authorized and required to issue to said C. P., in aid of the construction of said railroad and telegraph line, bonds of the United States of America of the denomination of one thousand dollars each, payable in thirty years after the date thereof, bearing six per centum per annum interest, payable semi-annually to the amount of sixteen, thirty-two, and forty-eight of such bonds for each and every mile of said railroad and telegraph line so completed and equipped as aforesaid, according to the character of the land or country over which the same might pass, that is to say : sixteen of said bonds per mile for seven and eighteen one-hundredths (7 18-100) miles from the city of Sacramento to the western base of the Sierra Nevada Mountains, forty-eight bonds per mile for one hundred and fifty miles across and over the Sierra Nevada Mountains, and thirty-two bonds per mile for six hundred and twenty-seven and 32-100 miles eastwardly across the Great Salt Lake Basin to Echo City aforesaid, in the Territory of Utah, amounting in all to twenty-seven thousand three hundred and eighty-nine 120-1000 bonds, of one thousand dollars each, and to the sum of twenty-seven millions three hundred and eighty-nine thousand one hundred and twenty dollars ($27,389,120) in value.

12.

That in and by an act of the Legislature of the State of California entitled " An Act to aid the construction of the Central Pacific Railroad in the State of California, and other matters relating thereto," passed April 25, 1863, and to which said act and every part thereof plaintiff refers as a part of this complaint, the Controller of the State of California was authorized and empowered whenever the railroad of said defendant, C. P., should be completed from the city of Sacramento in said State to the eastern boundary of said State, and ready for the conveyance and transportation of passengers and freight, to draw his, said Controller's, warrants upon the Treasurer of said State, and said Treasurer was authorized to pay the same out of the State Treasury, in behalf of and in favor of said C. P., in sums of not less than one thousand dollars each, for an amount equal to ten thousand dollars in United States gold coin per mile for each mile of its railway thus completed and equipped, and deliver such warrants to said C. P.

. 13.

That in and by that certain other law of the State of California entitled " An act to authorize the county of Placer to subscribe to the capital stock of the Central Pacific Railroad of California, and to provide for the payment of the same, and other matters relating thereto "—passed April 2, 1863, to which act plaintiff refers as a part of this complaint, the Board of Supervisors of said county of Placer was authorized, upon the affirmative vote of the qualified electors of said county so to do, to take and subscribe, for the use and benefit of said county, to the capital stock of said C. P., to the amount of two hundred and fifty thousand dollars, and therefor to issue and deliver to said C. P. the bonds of said county for a like amount, payable in twenty years from the date of their issuance, with interest thereon at the rate of eight per cent. per annum, principal and interest payable in United States gold coin.

That thereafter, and pursuant to said last mentioned act, a majority of the qualified electors of the said county, at an election duly held, did authorize the issuance and delivery of two hundred and fifty thousand dollars of said county bonds, as in said act provided.

14.

That in and by that other law of the State of California, entitled " An Act to authorize the Board of Supervisors of the city and county of San Francisco to take and subscribe one million of dollars to the capital stock of the Western Pacific Railroad Company and the Central Pacific Railroad Company of California, and to provide for the payment of the same, and other matters relating thereto," passed April 22, 1863, and to which said act plaintiff refers as a part of this complaint, among other things, the Board of Supervisors of said city and county was authorized and required, upon the affirmative vote therefor of the qualified electors of said city and county, to take and subscribe, for the use and benefit of said city and county, to the capital stock of the said corporation, C. P., to the amount of six hundred thousand dollars, and to deliver to said C. P. therefor the bonds of said city and county, to the amount of six hundred thousand dollars, payable in three years from the date of the issuance thereof, with interest thereon at the rate of six per cent. per annum, payable semi-annually; principal and interest payable in U. S. gold coin.

That afterwards, at an election duly held pursuant to said act, in said city and county, the qualified electors thereof did vote in favor of taking and subscribing for such stock, and the issuance and delivery of such bonds.

15.

That in and by a certain other law of the State of California, entitled "An Act to confer additional powers upon the Board of Supervisors of the city and county of San Francisco and the Auditor and Treasurer thereof, and to authorize the appropriation of money by said Board," passed April 4, 1864, to which plaintiff refers as a part of this complaint, the Board of Supervisors of said city and county of San Francisco was authorized and empowered to compromise and settle all claims on the part of said C. P., under the act referred to in the last preceding article of this complaint, upon or against the said city and county by reason of said act, by payment of cash, or the giving of other security, in place of the bonds authorized to be issued by said law passed April 22, 1863.

16.

That in pursuance of said last two mentioned laws, the said city and county of San Francisco, by its Board of Supervisors, did issue and deliver on or about the 21st day of April, 1865, to said C. P., bonds of the said city and county of San Francisco to the amount of four hundred thousand dollars, payable in thirty years from the date of their issuance, with interest thereon at the rate of seven per centum per annum, payable semi-annually in U. S. gold coin; and did at the same time relinquish to said company all claims in favor of said city and county, upon and against said C. P. for any of its capital stock provided to be issued by said act passed April 22, 1863.

17.

That in and by a certain other law of the State of California, entitled " An Act to authorize the city and county of Sacramento to subscribe to the capital stock of the Central Pacific Railroad Company of California, and providing for the payment of the same, and other matters relating thereto," passed April 25th, 1863, to which plaintiff refers as a part of this complaint, the Board of Supervisors of the city and county of Sacramento was authorized, upon the affirmative vote therefor of the qualified electors of said city and county of Sacramento, to take and subscribe, for the use and benefit of said city and county, to the capital stock of said defendant, C. P., to the amount of three hundred thousand dollars, and therefor to issue and deliver to the said C. P. the bonds of said city and county to the amount of three hundred thousand dollars, payable in thirty years from the date of their issue, with interest thereon at the rate of eight per centum per annum, payable semi-annually, principal and interest payable in U. S. gold coin.

18.

That in and by a certain other law of the State of California, entitled " An Act to aid in the construction of the Central Pacific Railroad, and to secure the use of the same to this State for military and other purposes, and other matters relating thereto," passed April 4th, 1864, and to which plaintiff refers as a part of this complaint, the C. P. was authorized to issue its bonds, from time to time, to the amount of twelve millions of dollars, ($12,-000,000) payable in twenty years from the first day of January, 1865, in U. S. gold coin, with interest at the rate of seven per cent. per annum, payable semi-annually; the payment of the principal to be secured by one or more mortgages on the railroad of said company, its rolling stock, buildings, machinery, fixtures, and corporate franchises, and the interest aforesaid to accrue thereon to be paid by the State of California.

19.

That in and by another law of the State of California, entitled "An Act granting certain rights to the Central Pacific Railroad Company of California, and for other purposes," passed April 14th, 1863, and to which plaintiff refers as a part of this complaint'; and also by certain ordinances and resolutions duly ordained and passed by the Board of Supervisors of the city and county of San Francisco and of the city and county of Sacramento respectively ; and by the authorities of other municipal bodies, bodies politic and corporate, in the said State of California, and in and by certain deeds of gift from said municipal bodies, bodies politic and corporate, and from divers individuals, duly executed and delivered to said C. P. as grantee, as plaintiff is informed, and believes, and avers upon and according to his information and belief, the said C. P. has acquired and now holds, and owns, and is possessed of, a large amount of real estate and other properties in said city and county of San Francisco, in said city and county of Sacramento, and at divers other places in the State of California and along the line of its railroad from Sacramento to the eastern boundary line of said State aforesaid, of great value, to wit : of the value, as plaintiff is informed and believes, and therefore avers, of ten millions of dollars ($10,000,000).

20.

That as plaintiff is informed and believes, and therefore avers, upon and according to his information and belief, and as certain other ordinances and resolutions duly ordained, made and passed by various municipal corporations and bodies politic and corporate of the said State of Nevada, and of the said Territory of Utah, and by various other deeds of gift duly executed and delivered by various municipal corporations, bodies politic and corporate, and divers individuals, in said State of Nevada and Territory of Utah, respectively, to said C. P., said defendant C. P. heretofore acquired, and is now the owner and possessor of, a large amount of real estate and other property in said last mentioned State and Territory, along and in the vicinity of its railway, of great value, to wit: of the value, as plaintiff is informed and believes, and therefore avers, of five millions of dollars ($5,000,000).

21.

That said Railroad and Telegraph Line, so as aforesaid authorized to be constructed by said C. P. from the Pacific Coast, at or near the city and county of San Francisco, in the State of California, to Echo City aforesaid, have been and now are wholly completed, equipped, and furnished, according to law, to wit: from Sacramento to Echo City, aforesaid, a distance of seven hundred and eighty-four and a half miles, or thereabouts; and the same, with all the franchises, privileges, and appurtenances thereto belonging, since the 8th day of May, A. D. 1869, have been and are now being operated by said C. P., and by the individuals, corporations, and associations hereinafter mentioned, for the conveyance and transportation of passengers and freights, and the transmission of telegraph messages.

22.

That all the bonds of the United States, authorized to be issued by said acts of Congress and resolutions hereinbefore mentioned and referred to, and the grants of public land thereby authorized to be made to the said C. P. by the said acts of Congress, and the said State bonds and warrants, and the bonds of the said county of Placer, and of the said city and county of Sacramento, and of the said city and county of San Francisco, and the grants of State lands authorized to be made to the said C. P. by the laws of the State of California hereinbefore mentioned and referred to, and the lands donated by the said city and county of Sacramento, and by the city and county of San Francisco, and by the various other municipal bodies, bodies politic and corporate, and individuals, as aforesaid, have all been delivered and made over to said C. P., and were received in its name by the said defendants, Leland Stanford, Hopkins, Huntington, Charles Crocker, E. B. Crocker, Marsh and Miller, acting as its Board of Directors, and the first and second mortgage bonds of said C. P., so as aforesaid authorized to be issued, have been issued by it and delivered to its said last named directors ; and all of said bonds, together with the interest coupons attached, have been sold and disposed of by said last mentioned directors in the name of said C. P., or are fraudulently detained by said last named directors ; and the moneys realized from all said sources and subsidies have been appropriated by the said directors, Leland Stanford, Hopkins, Huntington, E. B. Crocker, Charles Crocker, Marsh and Miller, and their confederates, to plaintiff unknown, and whose names, when ascertained, plaintiff prays may be inserted herein, with proper and apt words to charge them, to their own use, except such small portions thereof as were actually used in the construction of said road and telegraph line, as hereinafter averred.

23.

Plaintiff further avers, on and according to his information and belief, that under said acts of Congress and the acts amendatory thereof and resolutions supplementary thereto, in Articles 2 and 12 of this complaint mentioned and referred to, said C. P. became entitled to and has become the owner of ten millions and forty-one thousand six hundred acres of public lands of the United States, situate and lying between the city of Sacramento aforesaid and Echo City aforesaid, of great value, to wit, of the value, as plaintiff is informed and believes, and avers upon and according to his information and belief, of fifty millions two hundred and eight thousand dollars ($50,208,000) gold coin of the United States.

24.

That under said acts of Congress and the acts and resolutions amendatory thereof and supplementary thereto, there have been in fact issued and delivered to the said C. P., as plaintiff is informed and believes, and therefore avers upon and according to his information and belief, by the United States government, United States bonds bearing interest as therein provided, and payable at the times therein provided, to the amount of $27,389,120, to aid in the construction of said railroad and telegraph line, from Sacramento aforesaid to Echo City aforesaid; that said bonds now are and have been of the value, ever since the issuance thereof, in lawful money of the United States, of $27,389,120, and said last mentioned sum has been realized from the disposition thereof, and used and appropriated as hereinafter more particularly averred.

That pursuant to said law of the State of California, approved April 25, 1863, mentioned and referred to in Article 12 of this complaint, the said C. P., subsequent to the passage of said acts, and in the years 1864–5, received from the State of California the sum of $1,500,000 in United States gold coin, and which has been used and disposed of as hereinafter more particularly averred.

That pursuant to said Statute, approved April 2d, 1863, referred to in Article 13 of this complaint, the said county of Placer duly issued and delivered to said C. P. the bonds of said county to the amount of two hundred and fifty thousand dollars, gold coin, payable with interest as in said act provided, which bonds, when issued and delivered, were, ever since have been, and still are, of the aggregate value in gold coin of the United States of two hundred and fifty thousand dollars ($250,000).

That pursuant to said Statute, approved April 22d, 1863, and the acts supplementary thereto, referred to in Articles 14, 15, and 16 of this complaint, there were on or about the 20th day of April, 1865, duly issued and delivered to said C. P., bonds of the City and County of San Francisco, of the par value of four hundred thousand dollars, payable at the times and bearing interest as in said last mentioned acts provided, which said last men-

tioned bonds, when issued, were, ever since have been, and now are
of the aggregate value of four hundred thousand dollars, United
States gold coin, ($400,000) and that sum has been realized there-
from, by the disposition thereof, as hereinafter averred.

25.

That pursuant to said statute, approved April 25, 1863, referred
to in Article 17 of this complaint, the said City and County of
Sacramento duly issued and delivered to said C. P. its county
bonds to the amount of three hundred thousand dollars, gold coin
of the United States, payable with interest, as in said act provided;
and which said bonds, when issued and delivered, were, ever since
have been, and still are of the aggregate value of $300,000, gold
·coin of the United States, and that sum has been realized from the
disposition thereof, and used and appropriated as hereinafter more
partigularly averred.

26.

That pursuant to said statute, approved April 4, 1864, referred
to in Article 17 of this complaint, the said C. P. heretofore issued
its mortgage bonds, payable as in said act provided, with interest
coupons attached, payable by, and which interest has been, from
the date of said bonds to the present time, in fact, paid by, the
State of California. That said C. P. has heretofore, but at what
particular date or dates plaintiff is ignorant, sold or otherwise
disposed of said bonds, and has received and realized therefrom, as
plaintiff is informed and believes, and therefore avers, the sum of
$12,000,000, United States gold coin, which sum has been used
and appropriated as hereinafter more particularly averred. That
pursuant to the said Act of Congress, and the acts and resolutions
amendatory of and supplemental thereto, referred to in Articles 2
and 10 of this complaint, the said C. P. heretofore issued under the
signatures of its officers and its corporate seal, and delivered to

defendants, Leland Stanford, E. B. Crocker, Charles Crocker, Huntington, Hopkins, Marsh, Miller, and their confederates, to plaintiff unknown, its first mortgage bonds to the amount of $27,389,120, payable in United States gold coin, with interest at the rate of ten per cent. per annum, secured by the first mortgages of said C. P. upon its road, equipments, furniture, franchises, depots, machine-shops, and other property.

That, as plaintiff is informed and believes, and therefore avers, upon and according to his information and belief, the said C. P. issued and delivered on or about the   day of
186 , and on divers other days prior to the first day of March, 1876, to said defendants Leland Stanford, E. B. Crocker, Charles Crocker, Huntington, Hopkins, Miller, Marsh, and their confederates, to plaintiff unknown, its second mortgage bonds to the amount of $27,387,120, payable in United States gold coin, with interest at ten per cent. per annum. That said second mortgage bonds, with the exception of $11,787,378.17 of the nominal value thereof, and all of the said first mortgage bonds, have been, as plaintiff is informed and believes, and therefore so avers, delivered by the said C. P. to the said Leland Stanford, E. B. Crocker, Charles Crocker, Huntington, Hopkins, Miller, Marsh, and their confederates, to plaintiff unknown, and by them and their confederates kept and retained and appropriated to their own use, in violation of their duties as directors, in fraud of the rights of said C. P., of plaintiff and the other stockholders of said C. P. ; and said second mortgage bonds, to the amount of $11,787,378.17 have been sold by said defendants last above named, and the sum of at least $11,787,378.17 in United States gold coin realized therefrom by them, and by them or some of them converted to their own use.

27.

Plaintiff avers and charges that the following is a correct summary, statement, and estimate of the various subsidies and aids granted to said C. P. in aid of the construction of its railroad and telegraph line, as near as he can ascertain the same :

2

Value in gold coin.

Lands granted by United States $50,208,000 00
" granted and donated by various corpora-
tions, etc., situate within the State of
California 5,000,000 00
" granted and donated by various corpora-
tions and individuals situate within the
State of Nevada 3,000,000 00
" granted and donated by various corporations and individuals within the Territory
of Utah 2,000,000 00
Donation by the State of California 1,500,000 00
Bonds on which the State of California guaranteed
the interest 12,000,000 00
Bonds of. Placer County 250,000 00
Bonds of the City and County of San Francisco 400,000 00
Bonds of the City and County of Sacramento ... 300,000 00

CURRENCY.

Bonds of the U. S. Government $27,389,120 00
First mortgage bonds of said C. P 27,389,120 00
Second mortgage bonds of said C. P., delivering to
defendants L. Stanford, Charles and E. B.
Crocker, Huntington, Hopkins, A. P. Stanford,
Marsh & Miller, as above charged 15,601,741 83
Second mortgage bonds issued and sold as above
charged 11,787,378 17

Total $156,825,360 00

28.

That instead of undertaking by its own officers and agents the construction of its railroad and telegraph line, and the furnishing and equipping thereof, or making a reasonable contract with disinterested persons therefor, or letting out the work and the furnishing of materials for the construction, furnishing, and equipping thereof, to the lowest bidder; and instead of endeavoring to construct, furnish, and equip the same in the most economical manner, the said Leland Stanford, Huntington, Hopkins, Charles and E. B. Crocker, and their confederates, then composing a majority of the Directors of the said C. P., combining and confederating together to defraud the said C. P., and the plaintiff and other stockholders thereof, and to secure to themselves, jointly and severally, personally, great profits, advantages, and gains, entered into an arrangement among themselves, under the name of C. Crocker & Co., and under that name, from the commencement of the construction of its railroad at the city of Sacramento, until about the month of November, 1867, contracted with said C. P. to furnish the materials for, and to construct, furnish, and equip so much of said railroad and telegraph line as was constructed, furnished, and equipped, or partly constructed, furnished, and equipped, prior to the first day of November, 1867.

That such contract and contracts were caused to be made in the name of the said C. P., by the votes and direction of said Leland Stanford, Huntington, Hopkins, Charles and E. B. Crocker, and their confederates, (who composed a majority of the Board of Directors of said C. P.) with said C. Crocker & Co., a copartnership, of which the said last named defendants were members, for their joint and individual profit and gain, and the prices and rates at which the same were let were exorbitant and excessive, to wit, at the rate, as plaintiff is informed and believes, of two hundred per cent. over and above the actual and reasonable cost and expense of the work done, and the materials, furniture, and equipments furnished in the name of said C. Crocker & Co.; whereby the said last named defendants did receive from said C. P., and appropriate to their own use, and did vote to themselves, under the pretense of being Directors of said C. P., large sums of money, bonds, and assets of said C. P., to wit, as near as plaintiff can estimate the same, seven million dollars ($7,000,000) in value, over and above the actual cost of the work done and the materials, furniture, and equipments furnished in the name of, or under the direction of, said C. Crocker & Company.

29.

That afterwards, to wit, on or about the 18th day of November, 1867, the said defendants Huntington, Hopkins, Leland Stanford, C. and E. B. Crocker, and divers others, their associates and confederates, to plaintiff unknown, combining and confederating together to cheat and defraud plaintiff and the other stockholders of the C. P., and the said C. P., and fraudulently to acquire and appropriate to themselves, without consideration or a just equivalent, large profits and gains and large amounts of the assets and property of the said C. P., organized themselves and some of their servants and employees, to plaintiff unknown, under the laws of the State of California, into a corporation styled the " Contract and Finance Company," for the purpose of taking contracts for the construction of subdivisions of the railroad and telegraph line of said C. P. and the appurtenances necessarily connected therewith, and the equipping and furnishing the same.

That from and after the organization of said " Contract and Finance Company," all the contracts made and entered into in the name of the said C. P. for materials to be furnished for, and work to be done in, the construction, furnishing, and equipment of said railroad and telegraph line, were by said Leland Stanford, Hopkins, Huntington, C. and E. B. Crocker, and their confederates, composing a majority of the directors of said C. P., voted to be let, and in fact were let and entered into by said C. P., of the one part, and the said " Contract and Finance Company " of the other part, without advertising to let the same to the lowest bidders or bidder, and without in any manner inviting competition therefor.

That under the fraudulent and illegal pretense of paying for said materials, work, equipment, and furniture nominally contracted to be furnished and done by said " Contract and Finance Company," but really and in fact by said last mentioned directors and their confederates for their own benefit, the said last mentioned directors and their confederates from time to time voted to pay, deliver, and make over, and did pay, deliver, and make over, in the name of said C. P., to said " Contract and Finance Company " and its confederates, large sums of money and large amounts of bonds, lands, and other valuable assets of said C. P., of great value, to wit, of the value, as plaintiff is informed and believes, of two hundred and twenty-five million eight hundred and fifty-five thousand six hundred and eighteen dollars and seventeen cents ($225,-855,618.17).

That said last mentioned moneys, bonds, subsidies, lands, and other valuable assets so made over, transferred, and delivered to said "Contract and Finance Company," were in value greatly in excess, to wit, to the amount of two hundred and six millions six hundred and thirty-two thousand six hundred sixty-one dollars and fifty and one-third cents, ($206,632,661.50⅓) of the actual cost of, and of a fair price for, all materials, furniture, and equipments furnished by and work done by said "Contract and Finance Company," or by its sub-contractors or employees in the construction of said railroad and telegraph line, and the appurtenances thereof: and in said last mentioned sum in excess of the sum in which the same could have been let out for, and contracted to be done and furnished for, by responsible persons and firms who did not intend to cheat and defraud the said C. P., this plaintiff, and the other stockholders of the said C. P.

The said defendants, Leland Stanford, Huntington, Hopkins, E. B. and C. Crocker, heretofore, to wit, on or about the 20th day of July, 1869, under the name of said "Contract and Finance Company," divided among themselves the said two hundred and six millions six hundred and thirty-two thousand six hundred and sixty-one dollars and fifty and one-third cents, ($206,632,661.50⅓) in value of the assets, subsidies, and property of said C. P., so as aforesaid delivered to said "Contract and Finance Company," but in what proportions this plaintiff is ignorant, but is informed and believes, and therefore avers, upon and according to his information and belief, that the said sum was so divided in the proportion of one-fifth to each of the last named defendants.

And this plaintiff avers, on and according to his information and belief, that said "Contract and Finance Company" did sublet the greater portion of the work to be done, and which was done, and the materials to be furnished, and which were furnished in the construction of the said telegraph and railroad line under its contracts with said C. P. at prices greatly below, to wit, more than ten hundred per cent. below the prices which said C. P. nominally undertook to pay to said "Contract and Finance Company" for doing the same work and furnishing the same materials.

30.

Plaintiff further avers, upon and according to his information and belief, that all the bonds issued to the said C. P. by the United States Government ; also all the warrants issued by the State of California ; also the guarantee for the payment of interest by the State of California aforesaid ; also the bonds issued and delivered by the county of Placer, by the city and county of Sacramento, by the city and county of San Francisco, and the first mortgage bonds issued by said C. P. as aforesaid ; also the second mortgage bonds issued by said C. P. as aforesaid, have all been transferred to, and the control and benefit thereof vested in, defendants, Leland Stanford, Huntington, Hopkins, Charles and E. B. Crocker, and their confederates, under the pretense and pretext of paying and delivering the same to said "Contract and Finance Company," composed of said last named defendants and their confederates, as in part a fair compensation for the work purporting to have been done, and materials, furniture, and equipments purporting to have been furnished, by said "Contract and Finance Company" in the construction of said railroad and telegraph line, and the equipment and furnishing thereof, and the same have, by the said last named defendants, been converted to their own use.

31.

That the dividends, profits, and gains so as aforesaid received and realized by the said defendants, Leland Stanford, C. P. Huntington, Mark Hopkins, Charles and E. B. Crocker, and their confederates, in the name of Charles Crocker & Co., and in the name of said "Contract and Finance Company," amount, as plaintiff is informed and believes, and therefore avers, upon his information and belief, to the sum of two hundred and eleven million two hundred and ninety-nine thousand three hundred and eight dollars and seventeen cents ($211,299,308.17); the whole of which ought in justice and equity to belong to the said C. P., for the benefit of the stockholders.

32.

That defendant B. B. Redding is and has been, since the first day of January, 1865, an agent and employee of the defendants, Leland Stanford, Huntington, Hopkins, Charles and E. B. Crocker, though professing to be, and nominally appearing to be and to have been, during said period, an employee of said C. P.; that said Leland Stanford, Huntington, Hopkins, Charles and E. B. Crocker, acting as directors of said C. P., have, as plaintiff is informed and believes, and so avers, upon and according to his information and belief, heretofore voted to sell and convey, and have caused the officers of the said C. P. to convey, to said Redding and his and their confederates, unknown to plaintiff, a large part of, and the most valuable portions of, the lands so as aforesaid granted by the United States to said C. P. for mere nominal considerations, to wit, for one dollar and twenty-five cents per acre. That all of said pretended sales and conveyances have been, in fact, made with the secret understanding and agreement between said Redding and his confederates, and said Hopkins, Huntington, Leland Stanford, Charles and E. B. Crocker, and their confederates, that said Redding and his confederates should hold, and from time to time dispose of, said lands so conveyed to him and his confederates, as aforesaid, for the benefit of said Leland Stanford, Huntington, Hopkins, Charles and E. B. Crocker.

That said lands so conveyed to said Redding and his confederates are of great value, but of what value plaintiff is ignorant. That all moneys paid or purporting to have been paid, if any have been paid to said C. P. for said lands, have been, in fact, paid by said Leland Stanford, Huntington, Hopkins, Charles and E. B. Crocker, out of the profits and gains so as aforesaid made and realized by them in the name of the said "Contract and Finance Company" and in the name of said C. Crocker & Co. That there are divers other persons, to plaintiff unknown, who purport to have received, and have received, pretended conveyances of parcels and sections of said lands, the number of acres and particular subdivisions being unknown to plaintiffs.

That said last named persons hold the lands, so as aforesaid conveyed to them, in secret trust for Leland Stanford, Huntington, Hopkins, Charles and E. B. Crocker.

33.

Plaintiff is informed and believes, and therefore avers, upon and according to his information and belief, that said C. P., from its organization up to the 31st day of December, 1875, received for the transportation of freight, property, and passengers over its line of railroad to and from Sacramento aforesaid, the sum of fifty-five million one hundred and thirty-three thousand three hundred and sixty-four dollars and eighty-nine cents ($55,133,364.89) ; and during the same period, from the transmission of telegraph messages over its telegraph line, the sum of three million (3,000,-000) dollars.

That since the said tenth day of February, 1869, said C. P. has received for the transportation of freight and property (other than express freights as in Article 36 in this complaint mentioned) and passengers, the sum of five million nine hundred and seventy-three thousand and fifty-one dollars and seven cents ($5,973,057.07) ; and has, since said last mentioned day, received for the transmission of messages over its said telegraph line, the sum of two million eight hundred and seventy-three thousand dollars ($2,873,000).

34.

The plaintiff is informed and believes, and therefore avers, upon and according to his information and belief, that the first seven and 18-100 miles of said railroad and telegraph line from Sacramento, eastwardly, was actually constructed for a little less than eleven thousand five hundred dollars per mile. That the actual cost of the next succeeding one hundred and fifty miles, eastwardly, was less than forty-two thousand dollars per mile, and no greater sum was expended in the construction thereof. That the actual cost of the construction of the rest of said road and telegraph line, to wit, for a distance of six hundred and twenty-seven and 33-100 miles, was less than twenty-one thousand dollars per mile; which said cost for each distance included stations, depots, switches, turn-tables, side tracks, water tanks, and water stations, platforms, ware-houses, repair shops, machine shops, engine houses, and all other equipments and furniture of said road, except rolling stock. That the rolling stock, to wit, cars, engines, hand cars, and other equip-ments of said road and telegraph lines actually furnished for and actually used by said C. P., between its organization and the first day of January, 1876, has not cost to exceed the sum of two million dollars, and the plaintiffs charge, in fact, that the same has cost much less.

35.

Plaintiff further avers that he is informed and believes, and he therefore, upon and according to his information and belief, charges, that the said Leland Stanford, Huntington, Hopkins, Charles and E. B. Crocker, and their confederates, with the funds and assets of the said C. P., between the first day of July, 1861, and the first day of May, 1869, constructed and maintained a wagon road, commonly known and called the "Dutch Flat Wagon Road," and charged the cost of the construction thereof, to wit, one hun-dred and fifty thousand dollars, to the construction account of the C. P., under the pretense that the construction thereof was neces-sary for hauling freight and materials to be used in the construc-tion of said railroad.

That said Stanford, Huntington, Hopkins, Charles and E. B. Crocker, and their confederates, collected tolls on said wagon road, from freights, passengers, and vehicles passing over the same, to a large amount, to wit, to the amount of three hundred and fifty thousand dollars in United States gold coin, ($350,000) and appropriated and applied the same to their own use and benefit.

36.

That the defendant, Wells, Fargo & Co., has been, for ten years last past, and still is, a corporation duly organized, created, and existing under the laws of the State of New York, for the purpose of transporting express freight, coin, bullion, and other valuable packages and letters over the various lines of railroad and steamboat travel throughout the United States, and particularly from New York city, State of New York, to San Francisco, in the State of California, and places intermediate. That the said defendants, Hopkins, Huntington, Leland Stanford, Charles and E. B. Crocker, and their confederates, to plaintiff unknown, acting as and composing a majority of the Board of Directors of said C. P. between the first day of May, 1869, and the first day of April, 1870, but at what particular date plaintiffs are ignorant, in the name of said C. P., granted to and contracted with said defendant, Wells, Fargo & Co., in substance and to the effect, that said Wells, Fargo & Co. should have the exclusive right of running express freight trains, and carrying and transporting express freight, express packages, bullion, &c., over said C. P.'s line of railway; that in consideration thereof, said Wells, Fargo & Co. increased or "watered" its capital stock from $10,000,000.00 to $15,000,000.00, and delivered and made over to said Leland Stanford, Huntington, Hopkins, Charles and E. B. Crocker, or for their benefit, without any consideration, except the making of said contract in the name of said C. P., one and one-half millions of said watered stock of Wells, Fargo & Co.; and from thence hitherto, said Leland Stanford, Charles and E. B. Crocker, Huntington & Hopkins, have been, and now claim to be, the owners of one and one-half millions, or thereabouts, of said Wells, Fargo & Co.'s stock, of the value of $1,500,000.

37.

That the Western Pacific Railroad Company of California, on, and long prior to, the 13th day of December, 1862, was and ever since has been a corporation duly organized under the laws of the State of California, for the construction and maintenance of a railway and telegraph line from a point at or near the city of San Jose, Santa Clara County, California, by way of Stockton and intermediate places, to Sacramento aforesaid, a distance of about one hundred and twenty-five (125) miles.

That said last mentioned corporation, whenever hereinafter mentioned in this complaint, is designated by the letters W. P.

That said W. P. was, and is, by various laws and statutes, entitled to have and receive large subsidies in bonds, lands, rights, franchises, and other valuable privileges.

That as plaintiff is informed and believes, and therefore, upon and according to his information and belief, avers, on or about the 10th day of August, 1867, the defendants, Leland Stanford, Huntington, Hopkins, Charles and E. B. Crocker, purchased of one Charles McLaughlin and other persons unknown to plaintiff, but who composed the stockholders of said W. P., all the capital stock of said last mentioned corporation, and took and received a transfer and assignment thereof to themselves and their confederates, and at the same time took a delivery of, and there was delivered to them by the Directors of said W. P., so much of the railroad of said W. P. as had then been completed, and partly completed; and they have, since said day, controlled and managed the affairs and business of said last mentioned corporation, and have constructed and completed a railway and telegraph line from San Jose aforesaid to Sacramento aforesaid, and are using as the rolling stock and equipments thereof in running the same the rolling stock and equipments of said C. P. That the stock of said W. P., so as aforesaid purchased, was purchased, and said last mentioned railroad and telegraph line has been wholly stocked, equipped, and furnished, with the moneys and assets of the said C. P. wrongfully and illegally appropriated for that purpose by the said Stanford, Huntington, Hopkins, Charles and E. B. Crocker.

That said last mentioned defendants and their confederates hold said stock, so purchased, and said last mentioned railroad and telegraph line so delivered in trust for the said C. P. and its stockholders.

That afterward, to wit, on or about the 20th day of December, 1869, the said Stanford, Huntington, Hopkins, Charles and E. B. Crocker, and their confederates, received from the United States Government its bonds and coupons for sixteen thousand dollars per mile, for the distance from Sacramento to a point near Vallejo's Mills, in the county of Alameda, to wit, one hundred and twenty-five miles, as subsidies to aid in the construction of the railroad and telegraph line of said W. P. from San Jose aforesaid to Sacramento aforesaid, and have converted the same to their own use.

That such bonds when so converted, to wit, on the first day of January, 1870, were and still are of the value of two million dollars ($2,000,000).

That from the running and management of said last mentioned road and telegraph line, said Leland Stanford, Huntington, Hopkins, Charles and E. B. Crocker have heretofore received and appropriated to their own use large sums of money, to wit, three millions of dollars ($3,000,000) ; that said last mentioned bonds and sum of money, of right and in equity, belong to said C. P. and its stockholders.

38.

That said Stanford, Huntington, Hopkins, Charles and E. B. Crocker, with other moneys and assets of said C. P., so as aforesaid received, realized, and appropriated by them in fraud of the said C. P., and its stockholders, heretofore, to wit, between the first day of May, 1868, and the 20th day of March, 1870, constructed and equipped a branch of the said W. P., from a point near the Alameda creek, near Vallejo's Mills, in Alameda county, to a point at or near San Antonio, in the county of Alameda, and they and

their confederates now claim to own, and in fact manage, and
control, and are running, said branch in connection with the said
W. P., said C. P., and the San Francisco and Oakland Railroad
Company's road, hereinafter mentioned, and are and have been
receiving since September 1st, 1869, as net gains and profits of
running the same, about ten thousand dollars ($10,000) gold coin
per month.

That said last mentioned branch, its furniture, depots, and
equipments, and the net earnings there of, are, in fact and in truth,
held by said Stanford, Huntington, Hopkins, Charles and E. B.
Crocker, in trust for said C. P. and its stockholders.

39.

That the said San Francisco and Oakland Railroad Company has
been, for several years last past, and is, a corporation duly incorporated, and existing under the laws of the State of California, for
the purpose of running a railroad and ferry, and by means thereof,
transporting freight and passengers from San Antonio, Alameda
county, through Oakland, to the city and county of San Francisco.

That as plaintiff is informed and believes, and therefore avers,
upon and according to his information and belief, on or about the
20th day of March, 1869, the defendants Leland Stanford, Huntington, Hopkins, Charles and E. B. Crocker, and their confederates
to plaintiff unknown, purchased from A. A. Cohen, Michael Reese,
and others, the owners thereof, nearly all of the capital stock of
said last mentioned corporation, and the same was by said vendors
transferred and assigned to said last named defendants and their
confederates, and at the same time there was delivered to said last
named defendants and their confederates, by the Directors of said
corporation, the possession of the railroad, railroad depots, rolling
stock, furniture, and equipments belonging to the said San Francisco
and Oakland Railroad Company, and the ferry boats belonging to
it, to wit, the "El Capitan," and other boats.

That in consideration of said assignment, transfer, and delivery,
as plaintiff is informed and believes, and therefore avers, upon and
according to his information and belief, the said Leland Stanford,

Huntington, Hopkins, Charles and E. B. Crocker agreed to pay, and have, in fact, paid, to said vendors Cohen, Reese, and others, the sum of five hundred thousand dollars, ($500,000) in United States gold coin, which said sum has been and was wholly paid out of the funds and assets of the said C. P., so as aforesaid realized and appropriated to their own use by the said defendants, Stanford, Huntington, Hopkins, Charles and E. B. Crocker, as contractors as aforesaid, in the name of Charles Crocker & Co., and in the name of the said Contract and Finance Company, and as managers of the said C. P.

That said stock, so as last aforesaid acquired and purchased by said last mentioned defendants, is held by them in trust for said C. P. and its stockholders.

That the said last named defendants, by means of said last mentioned purchase, and since consummating the same, have elected their own confederates and employees and some of themselves directors of said San Francisco and Oakland Railroad Company, and have, since said last mentioned day, been running and operating said last mentioned railroad and ferry for the transportation of freight and passengers, in connection with said branch of said W. P., said W. P. and said C. P., and have received and realized as net proceeds of running the same about $30,000 per month, gold coin.

That out of the assets of the said C. P., the profits and gains of running the said branch and said San Francisco and Oakland railroad and ferry, the said defendants, Leland Stanford, Huntington, Hopkins, Charles and E. B. Crocker, have expended, in extending into the bay of San Francisco a wharf and pile track, in the direction from Oakland toward San Francisco, about the sum of nine hundred thousand dollars, ($900,000) and which extension was designed to be an extension of said San Francisco and Oakland Railroad, and is designed to connect the city of Oakland with Goat Island, in the bay of San Francisco, by a railroad.

40.

That the San Francisco and Alameda Railroad Company is and has been, for three years last past, a corporation duly organized, created, and existing under the laws of the State of California, and heretofore, to wit, on the first day of August, 1869, was the owner, possessed of, and engaged in running a railway, and transporting freight and passengers from Haywards, Alameda County, to the end of the Alameda Wharf, in said county, and from thence to the city and county of San Francisco by means of ferry boats by it owned. That on the day and year last aforesaid, as plaintiff was informed and believes, and therefore avers, upon and according to his information and belief, Alfred A. Cohen, E. B. Mastick, Charles Minturn, Edward Minturn, and F. D. Atherton were the owners of all the capital stock of said last mentioned corporation, and on the day and year last aforesaid, at the city and county of San Francisco aforesaid, contracted to sell and assign, and did sell and assign, to defendants, Leland Stanford, Huntington, Hopkins, Charles and E. B. Crocker, and their confederates, unknown to plaintiff, all of the capital stock of said last mentioned corporation, for some sum and consideration to plaintiff unknown, but which, upon and according to his information and belief, he avers to be, and to have been, for the sum of five hundred thousand dollars ($500,000).

That on the day and year last aforesaid, the railroad, rolling-stock, and equipment, wharves, ships, and ferry boats of the said San Francisco and Alameda Railroad Company, were delivered to and accepted by the said defendants, Leland Stanford, Huntington, Hopkins, Charles and E. B. Crocker, and since said day said railroad has been run, managed, and controlled by said last mentioned defendants for their own benefit, profit, and advantage, and they have received and realized therefrom large gains and net profits, to wit, ten thousand dollars ($10,000) per month, gold coin, and threaten to continue to run, control, and manage the same, and to appropriate the proceeds thereof to their own use.

That said last mentioned purchase was made and has been paid for, by said last mentioned defendants, with the moneys and assets of the said C. P., and with the moneys, gains, and profits so as aforesaid received, realized, and appropriated to their use by the said last named defendants and their confederates, under the names respectively of "Charles Crocker & Co.," and said "Contract and Finance Company."

41.

That as plaintiff is informed and believes, and therefore avers, upon and according to his information and belief, all the expenditures made in the construction of the said W. P. Railroad and Telegraph line, and said branch thereof, and in the purchase of said San Francisco and Oakland Railroad Company stock, and said San Francisco and Alameda Railroad Company stock, and in the construction of said hereinbefore mentioned extension of wharf and pile track, and all the expenses of running and managing said last mentioned railroads, ferries, and telegraph lines, have been by said Leland Stanford, Huntington, Hopkins, Charles and E. B. Crocker, and their confederates, charged to, and now are charged to, the construction account of said C. P., and to the running expenses of said C. P.

42.

That on or about the 25th day of June, 1870, the said San Francisco and Oakland Railroad Company, and the said San Francisco and Alameda Railroad Company, merged and consolidated their capital stock, debts, assets, and franchises, under the name of the "San Francisco, Oakland, and Alameda Railroad Company," with a capital stock of two million of dollars, divided into twenty thousand shares, of a par value of one thousand dollars each. That on or about the first day of July, 1870, the said Leland Stanford, Huntington, Hopkins, Charles and E. B. Crocker, being then the holders of nearly all the stock of the said San Francisco, Oakland, and Alameda Railroad Company, except about fifty shares thereof,

procured the acting President and Secretary of said corporation to
execute in the name of said corporation fifteen hundred bonds, for
the sum of one thousand dollars each, gold coin of the United
States of America, payable in twenty (20) years from the said first
day of July, 1870, with interest thereon at the rate of eight per
cent. per annum, payable semi-annually. And to secure the payment of said bonds, and the interest thereon, the said Leland Stanford, Huntington, Hopkins, Charles and E. B. Crocker, further procured the acting Secretary and President of said San Francisco,
Oakland, and Alameda Railroad Company, to make and execute
and deliver, in the name of and under the seal of said company
to D. O. Mills and William H. Tillinghast, trustees, a mortgage
upon all the property and assets and franchises of said company.
And plaintiff avers that said bonds are now held by said Leland
Stanford, Huntington, Hopkins, and Charles Crocker, and Charles
Crocker as the executor of the estate of E. B. Crocker, deceased,
who claim to be the owners thereof. And that the said last
mentioned defendants hold the same in trust for the said C. P.

43.

That the San Francisco and San Jose Railroad Company is,
and has been for the six years last past, a corporation created and
existing under the laws of the State of California, and having its
principal place of business at the city and county of San Francisco,
and is the owner of a railroad from the city and county of San
Francisco to the town of Gilroy, in Santa Clara County, together
with the necessary furniture, equipments, turn-tables, switches,
side tracks, depots, ware-houses, etc., connected therewith.

44.

That the Southern Pacific Railroad is, and has been for three
years and upwards, last past, a corporation duly organized, created,
and existing under the laws of the State of California, having its
principal place of business at the said city and county of San

3

Francisco, for the construction and maintenance of a railway from
the Mississippi river, by way of San Diego, to the city and county
of San Francisco. That under and by various laws of the United
States and of the State of California, mentioned and referred to in
Schedule B, hereunto annexed and made a portion of this complaint, the said corporation last mentioned has become, and is, entitled to large subsidies and grants of land of great value, to wit,
of the value of two million dollars and upwards.

That said defendants, Leland Stanford, Huntington, Hopkins,
Charles and E. B. Crocker, and David D. Colton, and their confederates, to plaintiff unknown, have by the use of means, moneys,
and assets of the said C. P., and the gains and profits so as aforesaid acquired by them under the name of Charles Crocker & Co.,
and under the name of said Contract and Finance Co., and not
otherwise, purchased and acquired, on or about the 20th day of
December, 1869, a majority of, and almost the entire amount
of, the capital stock of the said Southern Pacific Railroad Company.

45.

That immediately thereafter, and on or about the first of
March, 1870, with the intent and design of making said San Francisco and San Jose Railroad Company's road a part of the
contemplated railway to be constructed by said Southern Pacific
Railroad Company, from the Mississippi River aforesaid to the City
and County of San Francisco aforesaid, the said Leland Stanford,
Huntington, Hopkins, Charles and E. B. Crocker contracted with
the said San Francisco and San Jose Railroad Company and its
stockholders, to purchase in the name of the Southern Pacific
Railroad Company, and for their benefit, the railroad franchises,
privileges, furniture, and equipments of said San Francisco and
San Jose Railroad Company, and its capital stock, for a large
sum of money, to wit, three millions of dollars: and on or about
the first of April, 1870, as plaintiff is informed, and believes, and
therefore avers, upon his information and belief, paid to said San
Francisco and San Jose Railroad Company and its stockholders,

to wit, Charles Mayne, Peter Donahue, II. M. Newhall, and others to the plaintiff unknown, five hundred thousand dollars—part and parcel of said three million dollars—and have since paid the balance of said sum of three million dollars.

That said last payments were made by the appropriating thereto of the assets of said C. P., and the moneys, profits, and gains of said defendants, Leland Stanford, Huntington, Hopkins, Charles and E. B. Crocker, so as aforesaid acquired under the name of Charles Crocker & Co., and under the name of said Contract and Finance Company, and not otherwise.

That said defendant, David D. Colton, claims to be the owner of and entitled to some portion of the capital stock of said Southern Pacific Railroad Company, but of how much, plaintiff is not advised. But as plaintiff is informed and believes, and therefore avers upon and according to his information and belief, the said Colton has made no payment therefor.

That since said purchase, so as aforesaid in this article set forth, the said defendants, Leland Stanford, Huntington, Hopkins, and Charles Crocker have, as plaintiff is informed and believes, and therefore avers upon and according to his information and belief, by and through a certain corporation known as the "Western Development Company," constructed and built a certain line of railroad from Gilroy to Tres Pinos, about twenty (20) miles in length. And also have constructed and built a certain other railroad, from a point about one and a half miles south of Gilroy to Soledad, about seventy (70) miles in length. And also, a certain other railroad, from a point about six miles below Los Angeles to Anaheim, about twenty-one (21) miles in length. Also, a certain other railroad from Los Angeles to San Fernando, about twenty-four (24) miles in length. Also, a certain other railroad from Los Angeles, via San Gorgonia Pass to White Water, about eighty-five (85) miles in length.

And that the said Leland Stanford, Huntington, Hopkins, and Crocker are now engaged in extending such road to Fort Yuma, on the Colorado River. Also, a certain other railroad, from Goshen to Caliente—a distance of one hundred and fifteen (115) miles. All of which said railroads, in this paragraph set forth, are claimed to belong to and form a part of the said Southern Pacific Railroad.

And plaintiff avers, that all said railroads in this paragraph mentioned have been built by appropriating thereto the assets of the said C. P., and the moneys, profits, and gains of said defendants, Leland Stanford, Huntington, Hopkins, Charles and E. B. Crocker, so as aforesaid acquired under the name of Charles Crocker & Company, and the name of the said "Contract and Finance Company," and not otherwise. And that said roads are nearly all, if not entirely, operated by and with locomotives and cars belonging to the said C. P.

46.

That the Potrero and Bay View Railroad Company is .and has been for three years last past, a corporation duly organized and existing under the laws of the State of California. And heretofore, to wit, on or about the first of March, 1873, was the owner and possessed of certain line of street railroad in the city and county of San Francisco. And was also the owner of a long and valuable bridge in said city and county of San Francisco, known as Mission Bay Bridge, over which the cars of said last mentioned corporation run for hire. And that said corporation owns a franchise under which it is entitled to receive and does receive tolls for vehicles and animals passing over said bridge.

That on said last mentioned day, as plaintiff is informed and believes, and therefore avers, according to his information and belief, the said Leland Stanford, Huntington, Hopkins, Charles and E. B. Crocker, purchased all the capital stock of said corporation, and have ever since and do now claim to be the owners thereof. That the earnings of the said corporation since the said last mentioned day, amounting, as plaintiff is informed and believes, to the sum of .five thousand dollars per month, have been controlled and used by said last mentioned defendants for their own benefit, profit, and advantage.

That said last mentioned purchase was made and has been paid for by said last mentioned defendants with the moneys and assets of the said C. P., and with the moneys, gains, and profits so as aforesaid realized and appropriated thereto by the said last named defendants, under the names, respectively, of " Charles Crocker & Company," and the said " Contract and Finance Company," and not otherwise.

47.

That the plaintiff is informed and believes, and therefore avers, upon and according to his information and belief, there has not been any meeting of the stockholders of the said C. P., since the first annual meeting, at which the said Leland Stanford, Huntington, Hopkins, Charles and E. B. Crocker, and their confederates, were elected directors of said C. P., and ever since the second Tuesday of July, in the year A. D. 1862, the entire management and control of said C. P., its assets and subsidies, have been exercised by the last named defendants, secretly, and without having made any statement or statements of the receipts thereof, or of the true expenditures made by it or its officers, to the plaintiff, or to any stockholder or stockholders of said C. P.

48.

That the said C. P. is now under the management and control of said Leland Stanford, Huntington, Hopkins, Charles and E. B. Crocker, and their confederates, who compose a majority of the directors of the said C. P., and as they claim and assert, a majority of the stockholders of the said C. P., and who have refused, and though requested, still refuse, and said C. P. has refused, and though re-requested, still refuses, to institute this action, or any similar action, or make any inquiry into, or any showing of the disposition of, the earnings, assets, and subsidies of said C. P.

49.

That the San Joaquin Valley Railroad Company is a corporation, created under the laws of the State of California ; that with the assets of said C. P., so as aforesaid acquired by said Charles Crocker, E. B. Crocker, Leland Stanford, Huntington, and Hopkins, and their confederates, the said last mentioned corporation was organized, and said last mentioned persons have acquired a ·majority of its capital stock, and have procured to be granted to it large subsidies and gifts of land of great value, to wit, of the value of three million dollars ($3,000,000).

50.

That the California and Oregon Railroad Company is a corporation, created under the laws of the State of California, with the assets of said C. P., so as aforesaid acquired by the said Charles Crocker, E. B. Crocker, Leland Stanford, Huntington, and Hopkins, and their confederates, under the name of said Contract and Finance Company; and by the arts, devices, and fraudulent practices hereinbefore mentioned, said last named persons have acquired, and now claim to own, a majority of its capital stock of great value, to wit, to the value of two millions of dollars ($2,000,000).

51.

That on or about the 1st day of June, 1870, the said C. P. and the said W. P., under and in pursuance of the laws of the State of California, amalgamated and consolidated their capital stocks, debts, assets, and franchises, and formed a new corporation under the name of the Central Pacific Railroad Company, and that on the 20th day of August, 1870, the said last named corporation and the said The California and Oregon Railroad Company, and the said The San Joaquin Valley Railroad Company, and the said The San Francisco, Oakland, and Alameda Railroad Company, amalgamated and consolidated their debts, assets, and franchises, in manner and form as is provided by the laws of the State of California, under the name of The Central Pacific Railroad, and that said last named corporation assumed and became liable for all the debts and liabilities of all the corporations in this paragraph mentioned.

52.

That all the railroads which the defendant corporations, named in this complaint, were organized to build, and the capital stock of which, respectively, the said defendants Leland Stanford, Huntington, Hopkins, Charles and E. B. Crocker and their confederates, claim to hold and own, and have purchased and subscribed for, as aforesaid, with the moneys of the said C. P., appropriated by them as aforesaid, and acquired by them as aforesaid, in the name of Charles Crocker & Co., and in the name of said Contract and Finance Company, are and will be entitled to large and valuable subsidies, franchises, privileges, and properties. That the said last mentioned railroads and corporations have been organized and established, and procured to be organized and established, by the said Leland Stanford, Huntington, Hopkins, Charles and E. B. Crocker, while acting as directors of the said C. P. for their own personal benefit and advantage, with the moneys and assets of said C. P. by them misapplied for that purpose, and which in justice and equity belong to the stockholders of said C. P.

And said Leland Stanford, Huntington, Hopkins, Charles and E. B. Crocker, procured themselves to be elected directors of said last named corporations, respectively, and have procured for said last mentioned corporations, from the Congress of the United States, and by State laws, grants of large and valuable subsidies of lands, moneys, and bonds, with intent to appropriate the same to their own use and benefit, and in violation of the rights of said C. P. and its stockholders.

That in procuring said railroad companies to be organized, and themselves to become stockholders and directors thereof, and said subsidies to be granted as aforesaid, they have expended large amounts of money, to wit, one million dollars ($1,000,000) and upwards, moneys of the said C. P., and which in justice and equity belong to said C. P. and its stockholders. That the same was expended in lobbying and buying congressional and legislative votes and in perverting legislation in favor of their said schemes. That some of the coporations heretofore mentioned, to wit, said Southern Pacific Railroad Company, and said San Joaquin Valley Railroad Company, and said California and Oregon Railroad Company, have been organized and established by said defendants, Leland Stanford, Huntington, Hopkins, Charles and E. B. Crocker for the purpose of preventing all competition with other schemes conceived by them for their private emolument, and in fraud of the said C. P. and its stockholders.

53.

That the plaintiff has received no dividends upon the shares of the said capital stock of said C. P., so as aforesaid owned by him, although the plaintiff, as a stockholder, as aforesaid, has often requested the said Leland Stanford, Huntington, Hopkins, Charles and E. B. Crocker, composing a majority of the directors of said C. P., to make a settlement and declare a dividend from the assets of the C. P., after deducting the actual cost of the construction of the railroad and telegraph line.

The plaintiff avers that he is informed and believes, and upon and according to his information so avers, that a dividend of one hundred million dollars might be declared and divided among the stockholders of said C. P., still leaving a large sinking fund and surplus in the hands of the Treasurer of the said C. P., if said defendants Leland Stanford, Huntington, Hopkins and Crocker, and their confederates, would make an honest and correct statement and showing of the actual cost of the construction of the railroad and telegraph lines of the C. P., and deduct the same from the amount of assets, subsidies, profits, etc., of the said C. P., over and above all lands granted to it by the said United States and received by the said Stanford, Huntington, Hopkins, Charles and E. B. Crocker, in the name of Charles Crocker & Company, and the said "Contract and Finance Company," and divided among themselves.

That, although frequently requested, the said majority of the directors of the said C. P. have heretofore refused and still do re-

fuse to account to the said C. P. and its stockholders, in any
manner, for their actings, doings, and expenditures spent in furnishing, equipping, and operating the railroad and telegraph line of the
said C. P., or of the disposition made by them of the subsidies,
moneys, properties, earnings, and assets received by them in the
name or through the said C. P.

54.

That heretofore, to wit, on the
day of   the said C. P., by the votes of said
so claimed directors, Leland Stanford, Charles and E. B. Crocker,
Huntington and Hopkins, appeared to determine to, and did, execute and deliver to trustees therein named a first mortgage on its
road, telegraph line, franchises, rolling stock, etc., to secure bonds
to the amount of ($27,389,120) twenty-seven million three hun-
dred and eighty-nine thousand one hundred and twenty dollars.

That said mortgage was so executed and delivered, and said
bonds were so caused to be issued by said so claimed directors, as
though issued by said C. P., with the secret design and intent, on
the part of said Leland Stanford, Charles and E. B. Crocker,
Huntington and Hopkins, to secure said bonds to themselves, and
they have secured a majority thereof, to wit, twenty-two millions of
dollars, ($22,000,000), to themselves, without ever having paid
or delivered to said C. P. any money or valuable consideration
therefor, and now claim to own and hold the same ; that said Leland
Stanford, Charles and E. B. Crocker, Huntington and Hopkins, at
the time of voting as directors of said C. P. to execute said first
mortgage bonds, and at the time of forming the design of securing
the bonds to themselves so secured as aforesaid, formed the design,
and it is now their purpose and intent, as the holders of a majority
thereof, to foreclose said first mortgage and purchase said railroad
and telegraph line for their benefit, and thereby to defraud the
holders of the second mortgage bonds of the said C. P., to wit, the
United States Government and other parties and persons holders
thereof, to plaintiffs unknown, and this plaintiff and the other stockholders of said C. P. out of any dividends, benefit, or other interest
in said railroad and telegraph line.

That to the end aforesaid, and in carrying out said secret design and intent, among other things, said last mentioned directors entered into said contract with Wells, Fargo & Co. to run over said road, at much less rate than they charge other freighters and transporters, and also have concealed, and do now conceal, the actual running expenses of said road and its actual receipts. That said first mortgage purports to be, and said Leland Stanford, Charles and E. B. Crocker, Huntington, and Hopkins, assert and pretend that the same is, a valid and binding security upon said railroad and telegraph line, the franchises, equipments, etc., and that it was necessary to issue the said bonds and execute said mortgage to secure the same in order to construct said road. Whereas, in truth and in fact, the said several donations and subsidies hereinbefore granted to said C. P. were sufficient, and more than sufficient, to build and construct said railway and telegraph line without using any of said first mortgage bonds, and none thereof were used, in the construction, completion, equipping, and furnishing thereof, but, on the contrary, the same were fraudulently issued and delivered to said Leland Stanford, Hopkins, Huntington, Charles and E. B. Crocker, as said " Charles Crocker & Company," and said " Contract and Finance Company," and were and are wholly void.

That on or about the 10th day of April, 1870, one Samuel Brannan, being then the owner of 200 shares of the capital stock of the said C. P., and being about to commence proceedings by an action to compel the said defendants, Leland Stanford, Huntington, Hopkins, Charles and E. B. Crocker, to account to him for and in respect to the earnings of the said C. P., and the management of its affairs, and said defendants, Stanford, Huntington, Hopkins, Charles and E. B. Crocker, learning thereof, procured from the attorney of the said Brannan a draft and a copy of the complaint intended to be filed, and thereafter filed by and on the part of said Brannan.

That in order to cover up their fraudulent practices and business, and to still keep control of the said C. P. corporation, and to prevent the said Brannan and this plaintiff and other stockholders thereof from inquiring into and ascertaining the true condition of its assets, and the disposition thereof made by them, and to re-elect themselves as directors, the said Huntington, Hopkins, Charles and E. B. Crocker, and Leland Stanford, in the name of and by the agency of D. O. Mills & Co., and really for their benefit, since the said 10th day of April, 1870, purchased and had transferred and assigned to the said D. O. Mills & Co., 3,000 shares of the capital stock of C. P., so issued to the city and county of Sacramento, and said 2,500 shares so as aforesaid issued to said county of Placer.

That the said D. O. Mills & Company, although apparently the real actors in such purchase, were secretly acting therein, and were instigated to act therein by and for the benefit of said Stanford, Huntington, Hopkins, Charles and E. B. Crocker, the same last named persons; and upon the agreed secret understanding and agreement between the last named persons, or some of them, on the one part, and the said D. O. Mills & Company upon the other part, and to the effect that the said D. O. Mills & Company would hold the stock thus transferred to the latter, in secret trust for the said Stanford, Huntington, Hopkins, Charles and E. B. Crocker, or some of them; and would transfer the same to them, or some of them, when thereto afterwards requested; and would in the meantime cause the same to be used as should be requested by said Stanford, Huntington, Hopkins, Charles and E. B. Crocker.

That as plaintiff is informed and believes, and therefore charges and avers, upon and according to his information and belief, that in order to induce said D. O. Mills & Co. to appear to purchase the said 55,000 shares of said capital stock, and to secure said D. O. Mills against a loss, said Stanford, Huntington, Hopkins, Charles and E. B. Crocker, or some of them, deposited with said D. O. Mills & Co., or with some person or persons, to the plaintiff unknown, in trust for D. O. Mills & Co., $50,000 of the first mortgage bonds of the said C. P. corporation, and there now exists, or did exist, a secret and binding agreement between the said D. O. Mills & Co. on the one part, and the said Stanford, Huntington, Hopkins, Charles and E. B. Crocker, or some of the last named persons, on the other part, to the effect that the said last named persons would pay to the said D. O. Mills & Co. for said stock, the amount paid in advance by them to purchase the same, with interest at the rate of one per cent. per month on such advance when thereto afterwards requested.

That at the time said D. O. Mills & Co. purported to have purchased said 55,000 shares, they had been informed by the aver-
ments in the complaint of said Brannan as above set forth, and
had been informed thereof by the defendant, Leland Stanford.

55.

That some time in the year 1869, the said defendants, Leland
Stanford, Huntington, Hopkins, and Crocker, being then engaged
in a controversy with a certain newspaper, known as the "Sacramento Union," and published at the city of Sacramento, in this
State, for the purpose, as plaintiff is informed and believes, and
avers, upon and according to his information and belief, of injuring
and destroying the prosperity of said "Sacramento Union," established or purchased a certain newspaper in said city of Sacramento,
known as the "Sacramento Record."

That for the purpose of enabling said "Sacramento Record" to
injure and destroy the business and financial credit of said "Sacramento Union," and to prevent the "Sacramento Union" from
printing, publishing, and exposing the acts and doings of said defendants Stanford, Huntington, Hopkins, and Crocker, they, the
said last named defendants, advanced from time to time to the defendants William H. Mills, and the Sacramento Publishing Company, and other persons to plaintiff unknown, a large sum of money,
to wit, the sum of $200,000 in gold coin.

That on or about the 20th day of February, 1875, the defendants the Sacramento Publishing Company and William H. Mills
purchased the said newspaper known as the "Sacramento Union,"
and the good will and property thereof, for the sum of fifty-five
thousand dollars, and plaintiff avers that he is informed, and believes, and avers upon and according to his information and belief,
that the said sum of $55,000 was paid by the defendants Stanford,
Huntington, Hopkins, and Crocker.

That the said defendants, the Sacramento Publishing Company
and William H. Mills, claim to be the owners of said newspapers,
but plaintiff avers that the same are held in trust for said C. P.

That all the moneys so as aforesaid paid by said defendants, Stanford, Huntington, Hopkins, and Crocker, were paid from the moneys and assets of said C. P. derived by said last named defendants under the name of Charles Crocker & Co. and the Contract and Finance Company, and not otherwise.

56.

That on or about the 1st of January, 1871, there was a corporation existing pursuant to the laws of the State of California, known as the Oakland Water Front Company. The property of said corporation consisted of a large amount of property situated on the water front of the City of Oakland and the town of Brooklyn, and the town of Alameda—all within the County of Alameda—of great value, to wit, the value of five million dollars.

That plaintiff is informed and believes, and avers, upon and according to his information and belief, that the defendants, Leland Stanford, Huntington, Hopkins, Charles and E. B. Crocker, purchased from said Oakland Water Front Company one-third of the capital stock; and the same has been delivered by the said last mentioned defendants.

That the said purchase was made ·by said last mentioned defendants with the moneys and assets of said C. P., and with the moneys, gains, profits, so as aforesaid received, realized, and appropriated to their use by the said last named defendants under the names, respectively, of Charles Crocker & Co., and the said Contract and Finance Company, and not otherwise.

57.

That the Rocky Mountain Coal and Iron Company, of Wyoming Territory, was and is a corporation formed and existing pursuant to the laws of the Territory of Wyoming, having a capital stock of one million of dollars divided into ten thousand shares of one hundred dollars each.

That plaintiff is informed and believes, and avers, upon and according to his information and belief, that the defendants, Leland

Stanford, Huntington, Hopkins, Charles and E. B. Crocker, on or
about the first day of July, A.D. 1872, purchased, from persons
unknown to plaintiff, about eight thousand shares of the capital
stock of said last mentioned corporation, and now hold the same,
and claim to be the owners thereof.

That the dividend upon said stock has been, and is, eight thous-
and dollars per month.

That payment for the said stock was made by the said defendants, Leland Stanford, Huntington, Hopkins, Charles and E. B.
Crocker, by appropriating the earnings and profits of the said C.
P., and from the moneys, gains, and profits, so as aforesaid received
by said defendants in the name of Charles Crocker & Co., and in
the name of the Contract and Finance Company, and not otherwise.

58.

That the Los Angeles and San Pedro Railroad Company was,
and is, a corporation duly organized, created, and existing under
the laws of the State of California, having its principal place of
business at the city of Los Angeles, and on or about the last day
of February, A. D. 1873, was the owner of, and operating, a line
of railway about twenty-two miles in length, between San Pedro
and said city of Los Angeles, both in the county of Los Angeles.

The above said day and year last aforesaid, as plaintiff is informed and believes, and therefore avers, upon and according to
his information and belief, Henry B. Tichenor and others were the
owners of the capital stock of said last mentioned corporation, and
on the day and year last aforesaid, did sell and assign all of said
capital stock to defendants, Leland Stanford, Huntington, Hopkins,
Charles and E. B. Crocker, for and in consideration of the sum
of seven hundred and fifty thousand dollars, and that ever since
said purchase the said defendants, Leland Stanford, Huntington,
Hopkins, Charles Crocker, and Charles Crocker, executor of the
estate of Ed. Crocker, deceased, have controlled and managed the
same, and have appropriated the proceeds thereof, amounting to
twenty thousand dollars per month, to their own use.

That said last mentioned purchase was made, and has been paid for, by said last mentioned defendants, with the moneys and assets of the said C. P., and with the moneys, gains, and profits so as aforesaid received, realized, and appropriated to their own use by said last named defendants, under the names respectively of Charles Crocker & Co., and said Contract and Finance Company, and not otherwise.

59.

That the Market Street Railway was and is a corporation organized and existing under the laws of the State of California, and on or about the first day of March, A.D. 1870, was the owner of a line of street railroad on Market street, in the city and county of San Francisco.

That on said day and year last aforesaid, as plaintiff is informed and believes, and therefore avers upon and according to his information and belief, Henry M. Newhall, Charles and Peter Donahue, were the owners of all the capital stock of aforesaid last mentioned corporation, and on the day and year last aforesaid did sell and assign all of said capital stock to defendants Leland Stanford, Huntington, Hopkins, Charles and E. B. Crocker, for and in consideration of the sum of three hundred thousand dollars, and that ever since said purchase the said last named defendants have controlled and managed the same, and have appropriated the proceeds and earnings thereof, amounting to about five thousand dollars per month, to their own use.

That said last mentioned purchase was made and has been paid for, by said last named defendants, with the moneys and assets of said C. P., and with the moneys, gains, and profits so as aforesaid received, realized, and appropriated to their own use by said last named defendants, under the names respectively of Charles Crocker and Co. and said Contract and Finance Company, and not otherwise.

60.

That the Chesapeake and Ohio Railroad Company was, and is, a corporation formed and existing pursuant to the laws of the State of Virginia, for the purpose of constructing and maintaining a railroad from the James River to the Ohio River, about 400 miles in length. The plaintiff is informed and believes, and avers upon and according to his information and belief, that the defendant, Collis P. Huntington, on or about the 1st day of April, 1870, purchased a majority of the capital stock of said last named corporation, and claims now to be the owner thereof; and was then elected, and has ever since continued to be, the President and Manager of said Company.

That said defendant Huntington has, as plaintiff is informed and believes, and avers, upon and according to his information and belief, paid for, and in respect to, the interest which he claims to own in the last mentioned corporation, the sum of two and one-half million dollars. That such payment was made by appropriating the earnings and profits of the said C. P., and from the moneys, gains, and profits so as aforesaid received by said defendants, in the names, respectively, of Charles Crocker & Company and the Contract and Finance Company, and not otherwise.

61.

That on or about the   day of   187 , the said Central Pacific Railroad Company made and issued to the defendants, Charles Crocker and Silas W. Sanderson, Esq., as Trustees, 1,000 bonds, each for the sum of $1,000, payable in years from the date thereof, with interest at the rate of six per cent. per annum. And to secure the payment of said bonds, and the interest thereon, this said C. P. made, executed, and delivered to the said defendants, Charles Crocker and Silas W. Sanderson, Esq., as Trustees, a mortgage upon all the lands granted to said C. P. by the United States, in pursuance to the Acts of Congress in this complaint already mentioned and set forth.

The plaintiff is informed and believes, and avers, upon and according to his information and belief, that said defendants Leland Stanford, Huntington, Hopkins, Charles Crocker, Charles Crocker,
Executor of the estate of E. B. Crocker deceased, have and hold
said bonds, and claim to be the owners thereof; but that all the
said bonds are the property of the said C. P., and are held by said
last mentioned defendant in trust for the said C. P.

62.

That on or about the 10th day of June, 1874, the said C. P.,
having made large advances to a corporation known as the California Pacific Railroad Company, the said defendants Leland Stanford,
Huntington, Hopkins, and Crocker claiming to own and to be entitled to the sums of money so advanced by the said C. P., made an
assignment thereof to the defendant James B. Haggin. That
thereafter, the said Stanford, Huntington, Hopkins, and Crocker
caused judgment to be confessed by said California Pacific Railroad
Company in favor of said James B. Haggin, in the District Court
of the Sixth Judicial District of the State of California, for about
the sum of $1,309,041.84. That said James B. Haggin holds
said judgment in secret trust for the use of said Leland Stanford,
Huntington, Hopkins, and Crocker ; and that the same of right be-
longs to the said C. P.

63.

That the said defendants, Leland Stanford, C. P. Huntington,
Mark Hopkins, and Charles Crocker, have, since the incorporation
of the C. P., been acting as Directors and managing agents thereof. And as such Directors and managing agents, it is and has
been their duty to keep said C. P. in good and sufficient repair,
and to use the revenue thereof for such purpose. But instead
of so doing, and unmindful of their duty in this regard, the said
defendants have diverted the revenues of said company to the use
of the Southern Pacific Railroad Company, and other corporations,

and have allowed the tracks, bridges, culverts, water-ways, and superstructure of the said. C. P. to become in an unsafe and unsound condition, and in want of great and immediate repairs ; so as to render the same in many places unsafe for the transportation of passengers. And that the said works and superstructure of the said C. P., at this time, are in need of large and extensive repairs ; the cost of which repairs, as plaintiff is informed, and believes, and therefore avers upon and according to his information and belief, will amount to the sum of two million dollars and upwards.

64.

That on or about the 1st of May, 1871, the California Pacific Railroad Company was a corporation organized pursuant to the laws of the State of California, then engaged in running a line of railroad from Vallejo to Marysville, with some branch lines connecting therewith, and having a capital stock of twelve million dollars.

That on or about the said 1st day of May, 1871, the said defendants, Leland Stanford, Huntington, Hopkins, Charles and E. B. Crocker, purchased nearly all the stock of the said last mentioned corporation, and now claim to be owners thereof.

That said purchase was made, and has been paid for by said last mentioned defendants, with the moneys and assets of the said C. P., and with the moneys and profits so as aforesaid received and realized, and appropriated to their own use by the said last named defendants and their confederates, under the names, respectively, of said Charles Crocker & Company, and the said Contract and Finance Company.

That at the time of the making of said purchase there were issued by the said California Pacific Railroad, and delivered to said defendants, Leland Stanford, Huntington, Hopkins, and Charles and E. B. Crocker, 1,600 bonds of the said California Pacific Railroad, each for the sum of $1,000, made payable in 20 years from the date thereof, with interest at the rate of six per cent. per annum, payable semi-annually ; which said bonds are held by said last mentioned defendants in trust for the said C. P.

65.

That the Western Development Company is a corporation formed
pursuant to the laws of the State of California, for the purpose,
as plaintiff is informed and believes, and avers, upon and according
to his information and belief, taking contracts for building and
equipping railroads, and for the repair of such railroads as may be
controlled by the said defendants, Leland Stanford, Huntington,
Hopkins and Crocker ; and was organized for the purpose of taking
the place of the said Contract and Finance Company, so as to carry
on business of the same nature, and to enable the said last mentioned defendants to effectually conceal from this plaintiff, and the rest
of the world, their fraudulent and nefarious practices, done and per-
petrated through the agency and instrumentality of said Contract
and Finance Company.

And that the said Western Development Company is in fact owned and controlled by the said defendants, Leland Stanford, Huntington, Hopkins, and Charles Crocker.

And that all contracts given by said last mentioned defendants
to said Western Development Company, and all services rendered
by said Western Development Company, on or to the railroads controlled by said last mentioned defendants, are and have been paid
for at prices greatly in excess of their actual value ; with the intent to cheat and defraud this plaintiff and the other stockholders
of the said C. P. out of their proportion of the earnings thereof.

66.

That as plaintiff is informed and believes, and upon and according to his information and belief, charges and avers, the defendants, Leland Stanford, Huntington, Hopkins, Charles and E.
B. Crocker, have become and are the owners of large amounts of
valuable property in the leading cities and towns of this State, and
in many of the counties thereof ; and, especially, in the city and
county of San Francisco. The title to some of which property

stands in the name of the defendant Stanford, and some in the
names of the other defendants, or some of them ; and some in the
name of persons for the uses of said last mentioned defendants—
the names of said persons being unknown to the plaintiff; but
whom, when discovered, plaintiff asks may be made defendants
herein.

That as plaintiff is informed and believes, and so avers upon and
according to his information and belief, all of said property so held
by said last mentioned defendants, or either of them, acquired
since the first of January, 1862, has been paid for by said last
mentioned defendants with the money and assets of the said C. P.,
and with moneys, gains, and profits so as aforesaid received,
realized, and appropriated to their use, by the said last mentioned
defendants, under the names, respectively, of Charles Crocker &
Co., and the said Contract and Finance Co., and not otherwise.

67.

That on or about the   day of
                              1875, the defendants, Leland Stan-
ford, Huntington, Hopkins, and Charles Crocker, caused an application to be filed in the County Court of the County of Sacramento, praying for the dissolution of the corporation of the said
Contract and Finance Company.   And on the
                day of
1875, an order was made by said County Court, declaring said
Contract and Finance Company to be dissolved and disincorporated.
That said application and all proceedings had therein were made
without the knowledge of, and without any notice to, the plaintiff.
And plaintiff avers that said application was made, and that said
order was obtained, wrongfully and fraudulently, and for the purpose of cheating and defrauding this plaintiff, and of depriving him
of his just rights in the premises, and for the further purpose of
preventing him from having the evidence which the records and
papers of the said corporation would supply in support of this
action.

68.

That since the said defendants, Leland Stanford, Charles and E. B. Crocker, Huntington, and Hopkins became informed and advised of the contents of the complaint of the said Samuel Brannan, as is hereinbefore set forth, except matters contained in the foregoing Article 67, and that said Brannan intended to file said complaint, they, with the gains and profits made by them in the name of said Charles Crocker & Co., and in the name of said Contract and Finance Company, have purchased and secured to themselves a majority of the capital stock of said C. P., which was lawfully issued upon the basis of eight million five hundred thousand dollars ($8,500,000) capital, as hereinbefore mentioned.

69.

That plaintiff is informed and believes, and therefore avers, upon and according to his information and belief, that the said defendants, Leland Stanford, Huntington, Hopkins, Charles and E. B. Crocker are not worth, and have not in their possession or under their control, or jointly or severally are not the owners of property exceeding in value two hundred and fifty thousand dollars, over and above the property purporting to have been acquired by them, and of which they obtained possession and control, by misappropriating the assets and subsidies of said C. P., as hereinbefore averred.

70.

That as plaintiff is informed and believes, and therefore charges and avers, upon and according to his information and belief, said Leland Stanford, Huntington, Hopkins, Charles and E. B. Crocker, at the time they became directors of said C. P., were respectively comparatively poor men, that is to say: the said Leland Stanford was not worth to exceed fifty thousand dollars; the said C. P. Huntington was not worth to exceed fifty thousand dollars; the said

Mark Hopkins was not worth to exceed fifty thousand dollars ; the said Charles Crocker was not worth to exceed thirty thousand dollars ; and the said E. B. Crocker was not worth to exceed the sum of ten thousand dollars.

That none of the property of the said last named defendants, or either of them, was applied or used in the construction of said C. P. railroad and telegraph line, but the same has continued to be held and owned, and is now held and owned, by said last named defendants, respectively, as the same was held and owned at the time they first became directors of the said C. P., except as the same has been by them, respectively, exchanged for other property.

That beyond, and over and above, the capital stock of said C. P. and W. P., and the other railroad companies herein mentioned, the said Leland Stanford, Huntington, Hopkins, and Charles and E. B. Crocker have, by means of appropriating for that purpose the subsidies and assets of the said C. P., and not otherwise, acquired and now claim to hold and own, respectively, large amounts of real and personal estate of great value, to wit, of the value of two million dollars ($2,000,000).

71.

That the plaintiff has been wholly ignorant of the fraudulent devices, practices, and misappropriations of the earnings, assets, and subsidies of the said C. P., hereinbefore mentioned and averred, until about the first day of January, 1875, and did not, until said last mentioned day, know of, suspect, or believe, or have any cause to suspect or believe, any of the said fraudulent acts, transactions, and doings hereinbefore mentioned and charged upon the said Leland Stanford, Huntington, Hopkins, Charles and E. B. Crocker and their confederates.

72.

That the plaintiff is informed and believes, and upon and according to his information and belief so charges and avers, that as owner and holder of ten shares of the only capital stock legally issued, he is entitled to demand and receive, and have of and from the said Central Pacific, and from the said Leland Stanford, Huntington, Hopkins, Charles Crocker, and Charles Crocker as executor of the estate of E. B. Crocker, deceased, as plaintiff's part and portion of the profits made in constructing, furnishing, equipping, and operating the railroad and telegraph line of said C. P., the sum of about one million two hundred thousand dollars, and to fifteen thousand and fifty acres of land, so granted to the said C. P. by the said Acts of Congress.

WHEREFORE, The complainant prays the following judgment and relief, to wit:

First.—That during the pendency of this action, a receiver may be appointed by this honorable Court, to take charge of, manage, and run said C. P. Railroad and telegraph line, said W. P. Railroad and telegraph line, and the branch thereof hereinbefore described ; said San Francisco, Oakland, and Alameda railroad and ferries ; said San Joaquin Valley Railroad ; said California and Oregon Railroad ; and all the other properties consolidated under the name of The Central Pacific Railroad Company ; said California Pacific Railroad ; said Southern Pacific Railroad ; said Los Angeles and San Pedro Railroad ; said Market Street Railway ; said Potrero and Bay View Railroad ; and said telegraph lines ; and to discharge such other duties relative thereto as to this Court shall seem meet.

Second.—That during the pendency of this action, said Leland Stanford, Huntington, Hopkins, and Charles Crocker, and their confederates, be restrained and enjoined from acting as members of the Board of Directors of the said C. P., or of any of the other corporations in this prayer hereinbefore mentioned ; and that they be restrained from voting at any meeting of the stockholders of the said C. P., as representing any of the shares of the capital stock of the said C. P., and as representing any of the shares by them or either of them acquired since April 10th, 1870.

Third.—That the said Leland Stanford, Huntington, Hopkins, Charles Crocker, and their confederates, be restrained and enjoined from selling, transferring, pledging, or otherwise disposing of any portion of the stock of said C. P., or of any of the said railroad corporations in this prayer above set forth, or of the stock of said Wells, Fargo, & Co., or of the stock of the said Oakland Water Front Co., or of any mortgage bonds of said C. P., or of said California Pacific Railroad Co., or of said San Francisco, Oakland, and Alameda Railroad Co., or of said Southern Pacific Railroad Co.; or of the bonds issued upon said land grant, as in this complaint set forth; and of the stock of the said Rocky Mountain Coal and Iron Co., of Wyoming; or of the Atlantic and Pacific Telegraph Co., or of the Contract and Finance Co., or the Western Development Co.; or of any bonds heretofore received by said defendants, Stanford, Huntington, Hopkins, and Crocker, or either of them, for the use or benefit of said C. P., or any other of said corporations, defendant herein.

Fourth.—That said Wells, Fargo & Co. be restrained and enjoined from paying any dividends on its capital stock, so as aforesaid issued to said Leland Stanford, Huntington, Hopkins, Charles and E. B. Crocker, and their confederates, or either of them, as in this complaint averred.

Fifth.—That the said Oakland Water Front Co. be restrained and enjoined from paying any dividends on its capital stock, so as aforesaid issued to said Leland Stanford, Charles Crocker, E. B. Crocker, Huntington, Hopkins, and their confederates, or either of them, as in this complaint averred; or from making any transfer of any portion of the property of the said corporation to said last named defendants, or either of them, until the further order of this Court.

Sixth.—That the said Rocky Mountain Coal and Iron Company, of Wyoming, be restrained and enjoined from paying any dividends on its capital stock, so as aforesaid issued, to said Leland Stanford, Charles Crocker, E. B. Crocker, Huntington, Hopkins, and their confederates, or either of them, as in this complaint averred.

Seventh.—That any contract of sale, or any written agreement therefor, or any deed concerning the same, by which the lands, or any part thereof, granted by the United States to the C. P., have been passed, or are hereafter passed, into the possession and disposal of said B. B. Redding, be set aside as fraudulent and void.

Eighth.—That the said B. B. Redding and his confederates, the said Leland Stanford, Huntington, Hopkins, and Charles Crocker, and each of them, and their confederates, be restrained and enjoined, and the said C. P. and the said W. P. and all of the said corporations in this prayer above mentioned, and the officers of each of said corporations, be restrained and enjoined from selling, disposing of, mortgaging, or conveying, or contracting to sell, mortgage, or dispose of any of the lands granted by the United States to the said C. P. and said W. P. in aid of the construction of the said railroads, or either of them..

Ninth.—That each and every of the contracts purporting to have been made between the C. P. on the one part, and Charles Crocker & Co. on the other part, relating in any manner to the construction and equipment of the said C. P. Railroad and telegraph line, be adjudged and decreed to be and to have been null and void, and a fraud upon the said C. P., and upon the plaintiff and other stockholders of the said C. P. corporation.

Tenth.—And that each and every of the contracts purporting to have been made between the C. P. on the one part, and the said Contract and Finance Co. on the other part, and relating in any manner to the construction of the said C. P. Railroad and telegraph line, or repairs therefor, be adjudged and decreed to be and to have been null and void, and a fraud upon the said C. P., and upon the plaintiff and the other stockholders of the said C. P. corporation.

Eleventh.—That each and every of the contracts purporting to have been made between the C. P., or any of the railroad corporations, or either of them, hereinbefore mentioned, on the one part, and the said Western Development Co. on the other part, and relating in any manner to the construction of the said C. P. Railroad and telegraph line, or any of the lines of the aforesaid corporations, be adjudged and decreed to be and to have been null and void, and a fraud upon the said C. P., and upon the plaintiff and the other stockholders of the said C. P. corporation.

Twelfth.—That an accounting be taken of the actual cost of the building, construction, completion, and furnishing and equipping of said C. P. Railroad and telegraph line, and of said other railroad lines; also, the receipts and income thereof, from the time the same commenced running to the time when the receiver to be appointed by this Court shall take charge of said railroads ; and a fair charge against and upon said Wells, Fargo & Co., for the exclusive and special privileges so as aforesaid granted to them ; and also, an accounting of all sales of land acquired by said C. P. Co., and said W. P. Co.; and also an accounting of the disposition of all the stock of the said C. P.; of the bonds issued to it by the United States ; by said county of Placer ; by the said city and county of San Francisco ; by the said city and county of Sacramento ; of the bonds issued by it, the interest on which was, and is, guaranteed by the State of California ; of the moneys received by it from the State of California ; of the moneys received by it from the subscriptions to its capital stock ; the gains and profits made by said Redding, Leland Stanford, Huntington, Hopkins, Charles and E. B. Crocker, and their confederates, by the re-sale of lands which were heretofore belonging to the said C. P. and W. P., and the said California and Oregon railroad, and the said Southern Pacific railroad ; of the dividends received from said Wells, Fargo & Co.'s stock, and the stock of the Rocky Mountain Coal and Iron Co., of Wyoming ; and that in said accounting, the said Leland Stanford, Huntington, Hopkins, Charles Crocker, and Charles Crocker, the executor of the estate of E. B. Crocker, deceased, and B. B. Redding, and their associates and confederates, be charged with the gross receipts and amounts of all subsidies, moneys, bonds, and other assets received by the said C. P., and in its name, and be credited with the actual expenses only, at the fair cash value thereof, and the actual cost of constructing, of equipping the said railroad and telegraph line from Sacramento aforesaid, to Echo City, aforesaid ; such actual cost as was actually paid by said Contract and Finance Company, and by said C. Crocker & Co., without taking into account the profits and gains made by them, or either of them.

Thirteenth.—That the said Leland Stanford, Huntington, Hopkins, Charles Crocker, and Charles Crocker, executor of the estate of E. B. Crocker deceased, and Redding, and their associates, be adjudged to surrender to the said C. P. all bonds of the United States and of the said C. P. Co., and all of the stock of the said C. P. Co., by them or either of them held, or held by any person in secret trust for them or either of them.

Fourteenth.—That the newspapers known respectively as the "Sacramento Union" and the "Sacramento Record," and the good will and property of each and either of them, be adjudged to be held in trust for said C. P., and that the said defendant the Sacramento Publishing Company and the said William H. Mills be adjudged to account to said C. P. for the issues and profits thereof.

Fifteenth.—That the stock of the said W. P. and the bonds issued to it be adjudged to be the property of the said C. P.; that the stock of the said San Francisco, Oakland, and Alameda Railroad Co., and the bonds secured upon the property thereof, be adjudged to be the property of, and be transferred to, the C. P. aforesaid. That the capital stock of the said Southern Pacific Railroad Co., and the bonds issued by said company, and the lands granted to it, and the stock of the said San Francisco and San Jose Railroad Co., and of the said San Joaquin Valley Railroad Co., and the bonds issued thereon, and the stock of the California and Oregon Railroad Co., and the bonds issued thereon, and the lands granted to it—owned or claimed to be owned by the defendants, Leland Stanford, Huntington, Hopkins, Charles Crocker and Charles Crocker, Executor of the estate of E. B. Crocker, deceased, or either of them, and their confederates, or by any person on their behalf, be adjudged to be the property of, and to be transferred to, the said C. P.; and that all the lands and property mentioned in this complaint, and all lands and property which may be found to have been acquired by the said Leland Stanford, Huntington, Hopkins, Charles and E. B. Crocker, or either of them, since the first day of January, 1862, be adjudged to have been acquired with the property and assets of the said C. P. corporation, and be adjudged to be transferred to it. And that said defendants, Leland Stanford, Huntington, Hopkins, Charles Crocker, and Charles Crocker, Executor of the estate of E. B. Crocker, deceased, B. B. Redding, and their confederates, be adjudged to pay into the treasury of the said C. P. corporation the sum of one hundred millions of dollars. That said Wells, Fargo & Co. be adjudged to transfer one and a half millions of its capital stock to the said C. P. corporation. That the said Rocky Mountain Coal and Iron Co., of Wyoming, and the said Oakland Water Front Co., be respectively adjudged to transfer to the said C. P. corporation all the stock now held in said corporations by said defendants, Leland Stanford, Huntington, Hopkins, Charles Crocker, and Charles Crocker, Executor of the estate of E. B. Crocker, deceased, or standing in the name of any person or persons for their use, or for the use of either of them. And for such other and further relief as shall be equitable, and the nature of the case may demand.

ALFRED A. COHEN,
DELOS LAKE,
Attorneys for Plaintiff.

STATE OF CALIFORNIA, } ss.
City and County of San Francisco,

JOHN R. ROBINSON, being first duly sworn, says: that he is the plaintiff above named; that he has read the foregoing complaint and knows the contents thereof; that the same is true of his own knowledge except as to the matters therein stated on information and belief; and as to those matters, he believes it to be true.

JOHN. R. ROBINSON.

Sworn to before me this 15th day of March, 1876.

HOLLAND SMITH,
[SEAL.]   Notary Public.

SCHEDULE " A."—ARTICLES OF ASSOCIATION.

First—The name of the Association shall be the " CENTRAL PACIFIC RAILROAD COMPANY OF CALIFORNIA."

Second—The number of years the same shall continue is fifty years.

Third—The amount of the capital stock of this Company shall be eight million five hundred thousand dollars, divided into shares of one hundred dollars each.

Fourth- —The names of nine Directors to manage the concerns of the Company are: Leland Stanford, Sacramento; Charles Crocker, Sacramento; James Bailey, Sacramento; Theodore D. Judah, Sacramento; L. A. Booth, Sacramento; C. P. Huntington, Sacramento; Mark Hopkins, Sacramento; D. W. Strong, Dutch Flat; Charles Marsh, Nevada.

Fifth—The places from and to which the proposed road is to be constructed are the City of Sacramento and the eastern boundary of the State of California.

Sixth—The counties into and through which this road is intended to pass are Sacramento, Placer, and Nevada.

Seventh—The length of road, as near as may be, is one hundred and fifteen miles.

Eighth.—The names of five Commissioners to open books of subscription to the stock are: B. F. Moore, Dutch Flat; Edward J. Brickell, Illinoistown; E. G. Waite, Nevada; E. McLaughlin, Grass Valley; Samuel Cross, Sacramento.

Ninth—We, the undersigned, do hereby subscribe to the above Articles of Association our names, and the amounts of stock taken by us respectively in said Central Pacific Railroad Company of California: James Bailey, Sacramento; 150 shares. Mark Hopkins, Sacramento; 150 shares. C. P. Huntington, Sacramento; 150 shares. Charles Marsh, Nevada; 50 shares. Theo. D. Judah, Sacramento; 150 shares. D. W. Strong, Dutch Flat; 50 shares. N. W. Blanchard, Dutch Flat; 10 shares. C. Cole, Sacramento; 10 shares. John F. Morse, Sacramento; 5 shares. P. H. Russell, Sacramento; 5 shares. N. L. Drew, Sacramento; 5 shares. Wm. G. English, Sacramento; 10 shares. Chas. G. Hooker, Sacramento; 10 shares. Millikin Bros., Sacramento; 10 shares. Lord, Holbrook & Co., Sacramento; 10 shares. Lucius A. Booth, Sacramento; 10 shares. E. J. Brickell, Illinoistown; 40 shares. B. Brickell, Illinoistown; 20 shares. B. F. Moore, Dutch Flat; 10 shares. P. T. Mathewson, Dutch Flat, 5 shares. E. L. Bradley and R. M. Trim, Dutch Flat; 25 shares. E. G. Waite, Nevada; 10 shares. John Williams, Nevada; 10 shares. T. Ellard Beans, Nevada; 10 shares. J. N. Lumay, Nevada; 10 shares. E. McLaughlin, Grass Valley; 10 shares. Wm. Loutzenheim, Grass Valley; 5 shares. Leland Stanford, Sacramento; 150 shares. O. Crocker, Sacramento; 150 shares. Samuel Cross, Sacramento; 10 shares. Total, 1,250 shares.

STATE OF CALIFORNIA, } ss.
City and County of Sacramento,

Be it remembered, that on this 27th day of June, 1861, personally appeared before the undersigned, a notary public in and for said city and county, Leland Stanford, Mark Hopkins, and C. P. Huntington, three of the directors of the within named Central Pacific Railroad Company of California, and being by me duly sworn, say: That the stock to the amount of at least one thousand dollars for every mile of the railroad intended to be built by said company, to wit, an amount of stock exceeding one hundred and fifteen thousand dollars, has been in good faith subscribed by the members of said company, and that ten per cent. on the amount of stock subscribed as aforesaid has been actually, and in good faith, paid in cash to Mark Hopkins, the Treasurer appointed by the Directors named in the within articles of association, and that the subscribers are all known by some one of said affiants to be subscribers thereto, and to be the persons so represented.

LELAND STANFORD,
MARK HOPKINS,
C. P. HUNTINGTON.

I hereby certify that the foregoing affidavit was duly subscribed and sworn to by said Leland Stanford, Mark Hopkins, and C. P. Huntington, by and before me, the day and year aforesaid.

In testimony whereof, I have hereunto set my hand and official seal, this 27th day of June, A. D. 1861.

[SEAL.]   ELIJAH SWIFT, Notary Public.

[63]

SCHEDULE "B."

By the Act of Congress of July 27, 1866, incorporating the Atlantic and Pacific Railroad Company, there is granted to the defendant, the Southern Pacific Railroad Company—

SEC. 3. "Every alternate section of public land, not mineral, designated by odd numbers, to the amount of twenty alternate sections per mile, on each side of said railroad line," *provided*, if the route shall be found upon the line of any other railroad to construct which Congress has granted lands, as far as " the routes are upon the same general line, the amount heretofore granted shall be deducted from the amount granted by this Act." (Acts 1st Sess. 39th Cong., 1866, p. 304.)

By Act of Legislature of California, 30 acres tide lands in San Francisco Bay ; value, $500,000.

www.ingramcontent.com/pod-product-compliance
Lightning Source LLC
Chambersburg PA
CBHW021628270326
41931CB00008B/914